はしがき

　嵌め込み式遮蔽形体は、屋外と屋内を遮蔽するガラス戸においては、半透明な断熱材を使用し、一部開閉自在として、屋外が見えるように構成されているものである。これにより、外気との断熱効果を発揮し、省エネとなる。また、屋内においての障子戸の仕切りでは、冷房・暖房の断熱効果を発揮し、省エネ効果となるものである。

Preface

In the glass door which covers the room outside, translucent thermal insulation is used for insertion type cover form, and as opening and closing being free in part, it is constituted so that the outdoors can be seen.

Thereby, an adiabatic effect with the open air is demonstrated and it becomes energy saving.

Moreover, with an indoor shoji, the adiabatic effect of air conditioning and heating is demonstrated, and it becomes an energy-saving effect.

目　次

1、嵌め込み式遮蔽形体の用途解説（イラスト解説）

(1) 縁側雨戸 -- 7

(2) テラスの雨戸 -- 8

(3) 窓の雨戸 -- 9

(4) 障子戸の枠 --- 10

(5) 窓 -- 11

(6) 組み込み窓 --- 12

(7) アルミサッシ引き戸 -- 13

(8) 上下開閉窓 --- 14

(9) 強力削減"熱気や冷気も"省エネ -- 15

2、英語解説

Use description of an insertion type cover form (illustration description)

(1) -- 17

Veranda sliding shutter

(2) -- 18

The sliding shutter of a terrace

(3) -- 19

The sliding shutter of a window

(4) -- 20

The frame of a shoji door

(5) -- 21

Window

(6) ---22

Inclusion window

(7) ---23

Aluminum sash sliding door

(8) ---24

Up-and-down opening-and-closing window

(9) ---25

powerful reduction "heat and cold" -- energy is saved

3、中国語解说

镶嵌式遮蔽零件的用途解说(插图解说)

(1) ---26

廊子滑窗

(2) ---27

阳台的滑窗

(3) ---28

窗的滑窗

(4) ---29

拉门

(5) ---30

窗

(6) ---31

安装窗

(7) --32

铝框格拉门

(8) --33

上下开闭窗

(9) --34

强有力的削减"热气以及冷气"是节能

4、公报解说--35

5、Patent journal English ------------------------------41

１、嵌め込み式遮蔽形体の用途解説（（イラスト解説）

⑴　縁側雨戸

　　縁側のガラス戸の内側から半透明の断熱材を嵌合し、明るさを低下させない。

　　また一部分を開閉にし、外が見れるようにする。

⑵ テラスの雨戸

　雨戸の内側から断熱材を嵌着。

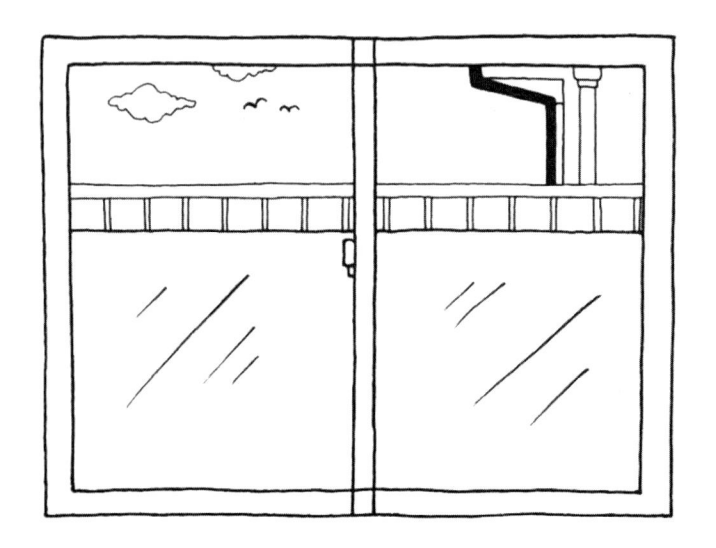

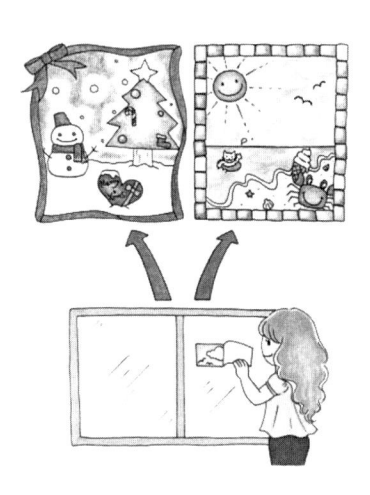

(3) **窓の雨戸**

雨戸の内側から断熱材を嵌着。

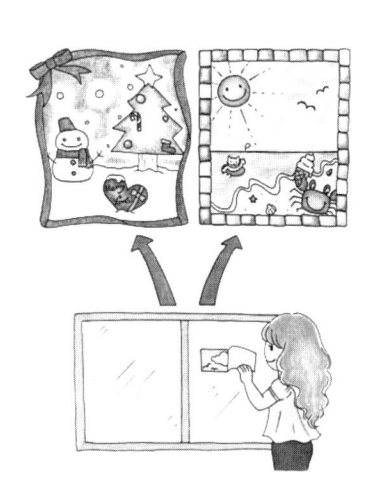

⑷ 障子戸の枠

　障子戸の内側から半透明な断熱材を嵌合し、明るさを低下させない。

⑸ 窓

　窓のガラス戸の内側から断熱材を着脱自在に嵌合させ、一部分を開閉にし、外が見れるようにする。

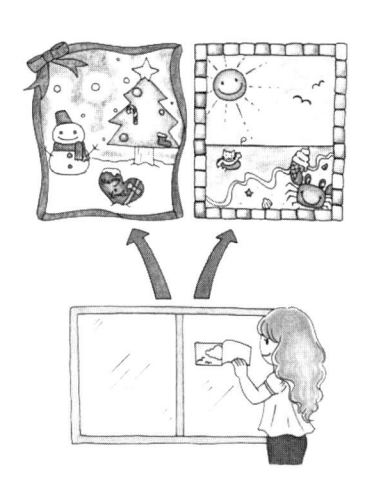

⑹ 組み込み窓

組み込み式の開閉窓に内側から断熱材を嵌着。

(7) アルミサッシ引き戸

　ガラスの部分に内側から一部開閉自在な断熱シートを嵌着

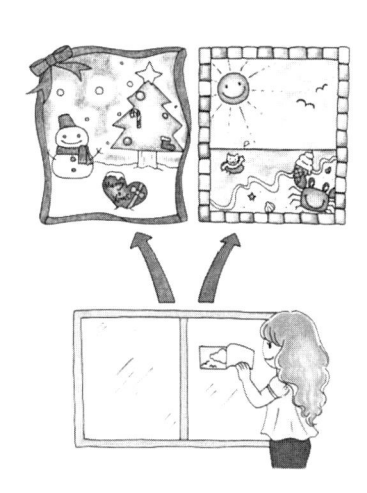

⑻　上下開閉窓

　ガラスの部分に内側から一部開閉自在な断熱シートを嵌着

(9) 強力削減 "熱気や冷気も" 省エネ

雨戸やガラス戸や障子戸等を通して室外からの直射日光や熱気や冷気等が室内の温度環境の悪化に影響することを低減させ、省エネに役立つ遮蔽形体を提供する。

　雨戸やガラス戸や障子戸等の室内側の空きスペースに断熱体1をはめ込むことより成り、断熱体が冷暖熱を遮蔽する効果を利用することにより、室内への温度環境の悪化を低減させることを特徴とする。

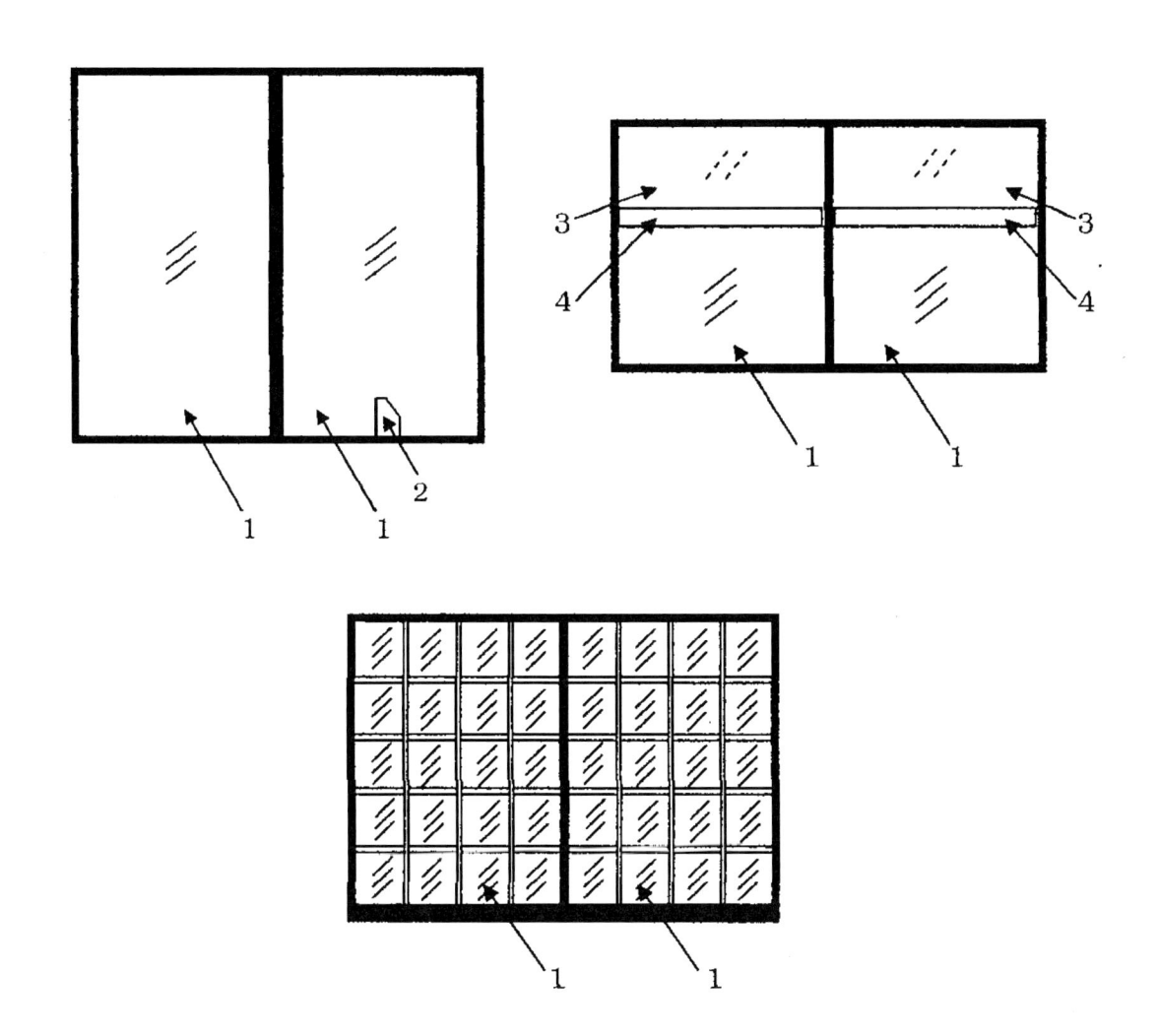

２、英語解説

Use description of an insertion type cover form (illustration description)

(1)

Veranda sliding shutter

Fitting of the translucent thermal insulation is carried out from the inner side of the glass door of a veranda, and brightness is not reduced.

Moreover, a part is made opening and closing and it can be made for outside to see.

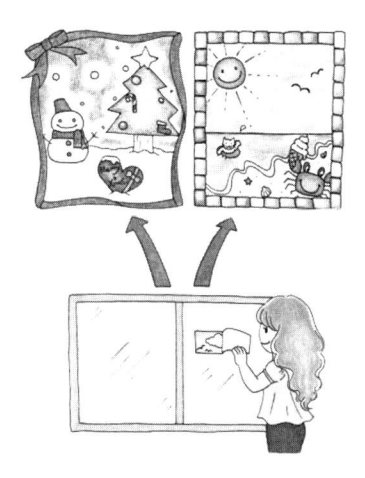

(2)

The sliding shutter of a terrace

Thermal insulation is inserted in from the inner side of a sliding shutter.

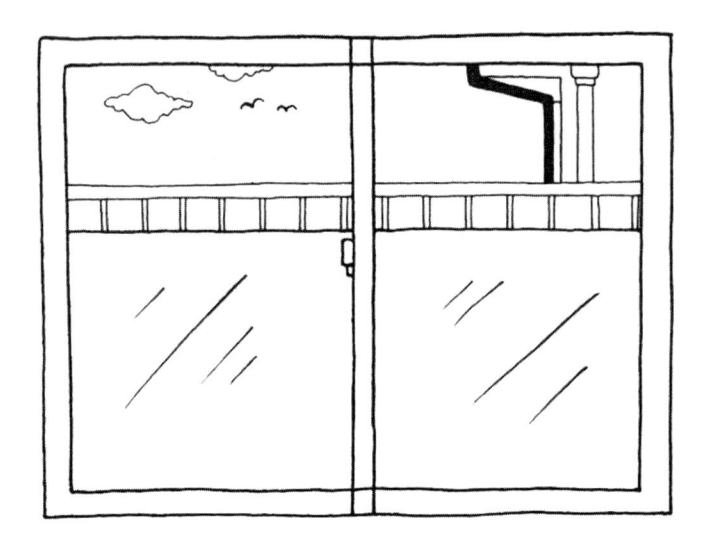

(3)

The sliding shutter of a window

Thermal insulation is inserted in from the inner side of a sliding shutter.

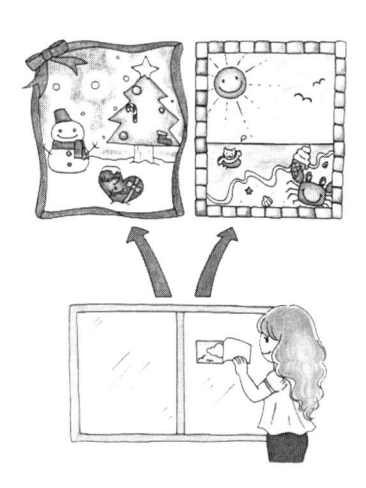

(4)

The frame of a shoji door

Fitting of the translucent thermal insulation is carried out from the inner side of a shoji door, and brightness is not reduced.

(5)

Window

Fitting of the attachment and detachment of thermal insulation is made free from the inner side of the glass door of a window, a part is made opening and closing, and it can be made for outside to see.

21

(6)

Inclusion window

It is insertion about an inner side to thermal insulation to a fixed opening-and-closing window.

(7)

Aluminum sash sliding door

It is insertion from an inner side in part to the portion of glass about the heat insulation sheet which can be opened and closed freely.

(8)

Up-and-down opening-and-closing window

The heat insulation sheet which can be opened and closed freely is inserted in the portion of glass in part from an inner side.

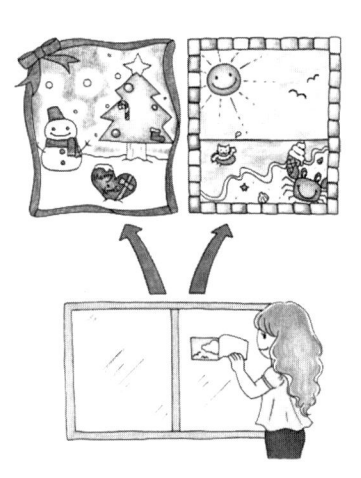

powerful reduction "heat and cold" -- energy is saved

It reduces that the direct rays and the heat from outdoor, cold, etc. affect aggravation of indoor temperature environment through a sliding shutter, a glass door, a shoji door, etc., and offers the cover form which is useful for energy saving.

It is characterized by reducing aggravation of the temperature environment to the interior of a room by consisting of inserting the heat insulation object 1 in the free space on the interior-of-a-room side, such as a sliding shutter, a glass door, and a shoji door, and using the effect which a heat insulation object covers.

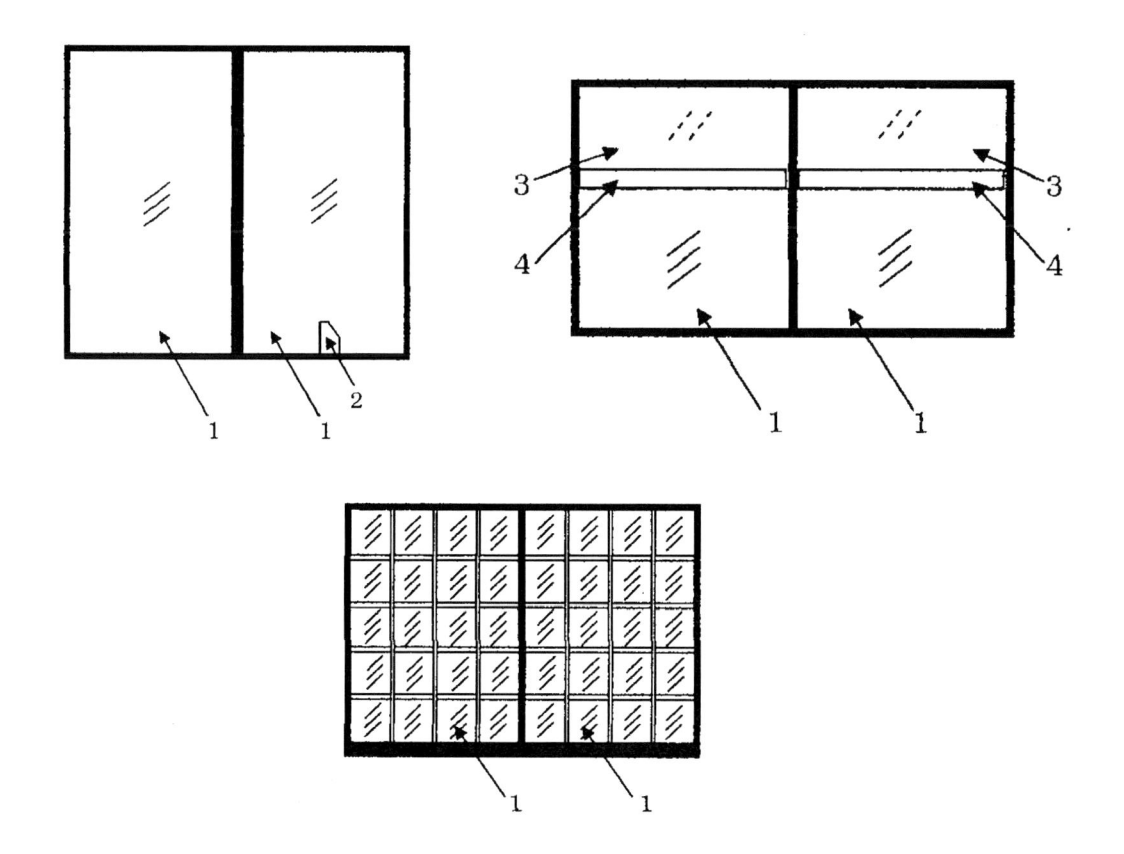

２、中国語解说

镶嵌式遮蔽零件的用途解说（插图解说）

(1)

廊子滑窗

从廊子的玻璃门的內侧做嵌合半透明的隔热材料,不使明亮降低。 另外,把一部分换成开闭,能看外部。

(2)

阳台的滑窗

用隔热材料从滑窗的内侧是嵌着。

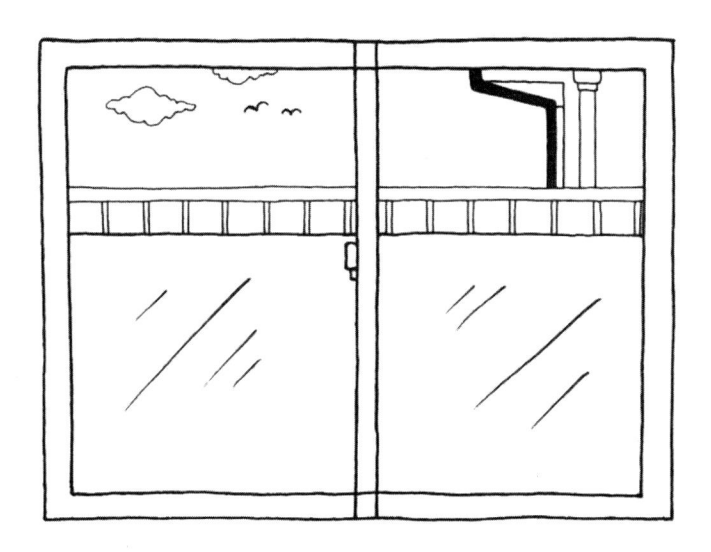

⑶

窗的滑窗

用隔热材料从滑窗的内侧是嵌着。

(4)

拉门

从拉门门的内侧做嵌合半透明的隔热材料,不使明亮降低。

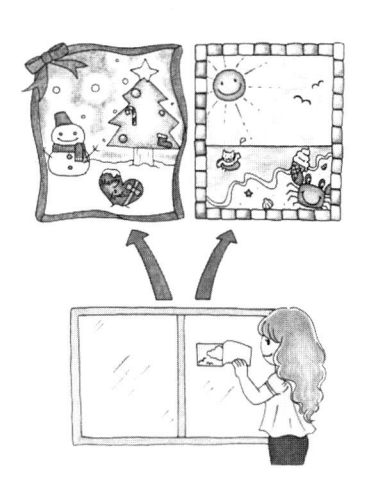

(5)

窗

从窗的玻璃门的内侧戴上隔热材料,为了能看外部把一部分换成开闭。

(6)

安装窗

用隔热材料从内侧对安装式开闭窗是嵌着。

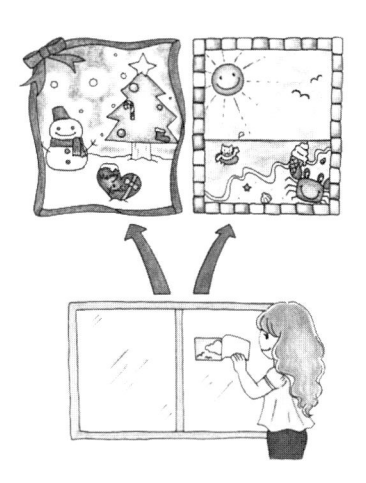

31

(7)

铝框格拉门

用开闭从内侧对玻璃的部分一部分自在的断热席是嵌着

32

⑻

上下开闭窗

用开闭从内侧对玻璃的部分一部分自在的断热席是嵌着

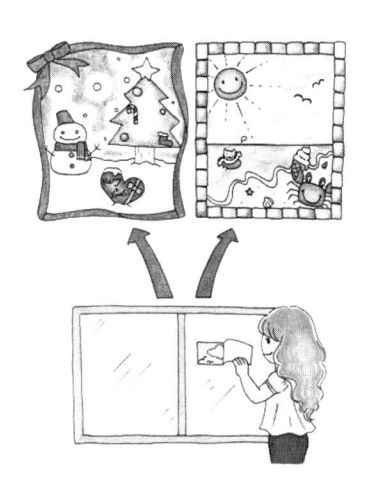

(9)

强有力的削减"热气以及冷气"是节能

强有力的削减"热气以及冷气"是节能

让减少始自于室外的直射日光以及热气或者冷气通过滑窗以及玻璃门或者拉门门影响室内的温度环境的恶化的,提供在节能有用的遮蔽形态。

构成由断热身体1往嵌入的,为特征以让因为利用断热身体遮掩的效果所以减少到室内的温度环境的恶化的。

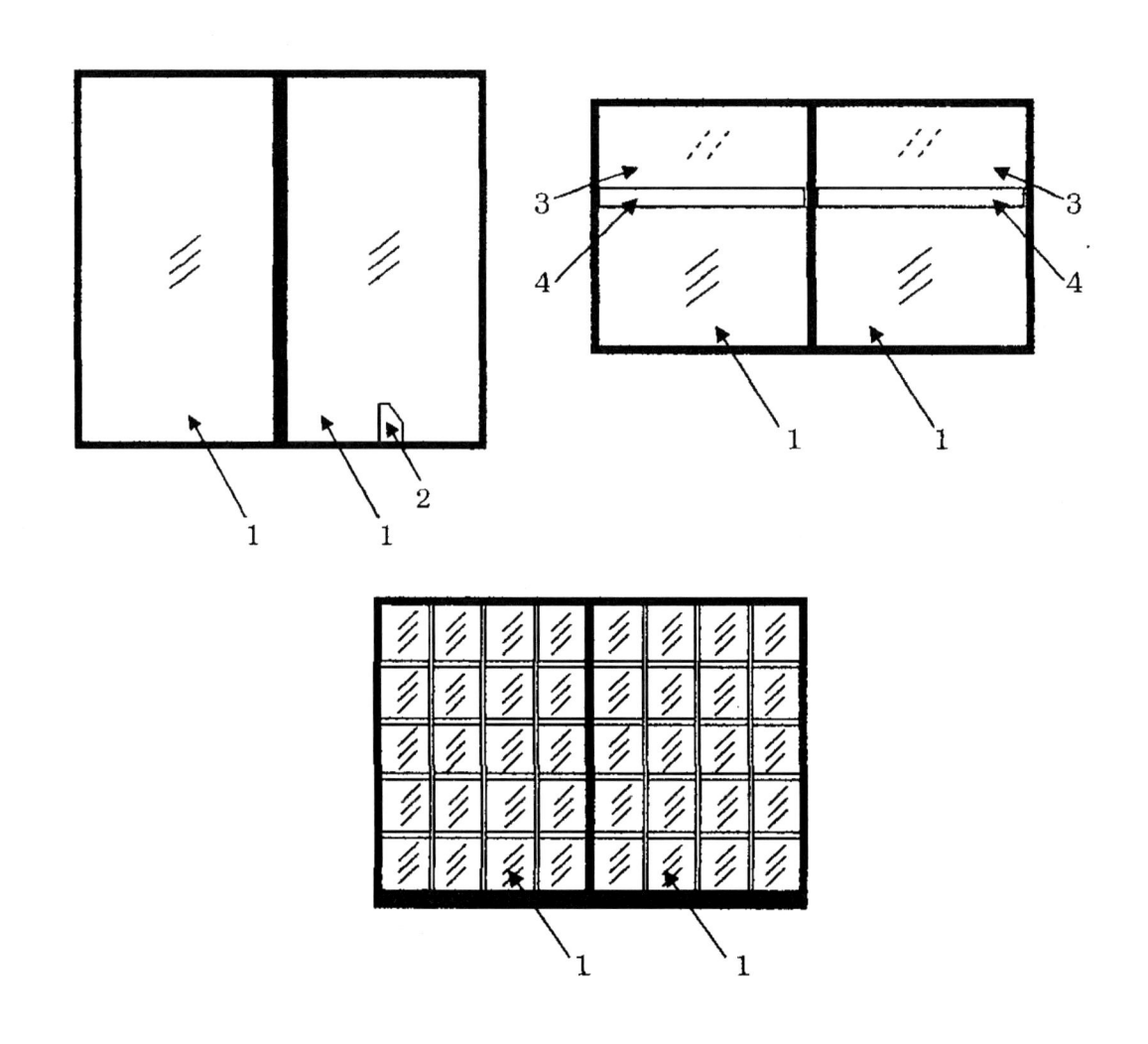

４、公報解説

実用新案登録第３１８４４０１号

考案の名称；遮蔽形体

実用新案権者；松岡　正

【要約】

【課題】雨戸やガラス戸や障子戸等を通して室外からの直射日光や熱気や冷気等が室内の温度環境の悪化に影響することを低減させ、省エネに役立つ遮蔽形体を提供する。

【解決手段】雨戸やガラス戸や障子戸等の室内側の空きスペースに断熱体1をはめ込むことより成り、断熱体が冷暖熱を遮蔽する効果を利用することにより、室内への温度環境の悪化を低減させることを特徴とする。

【選択図】図１

【実用新案登録請求の範囲】

【請求項１】

雨戸やガラス戸や障子戸等の室内側の空きスペースに断熱体をはめ込むことにより成り、断熱体が冷暖熱を遮蔽する効果を利用することにより、室内への温度環境の悪化を低減させることを特徴とする遮蔽形体。

【考案の詳細な説明】

【利用分野】

【０００１】

本考案は、日よけや熱気や冷気等を防ぎ、室内の温度環境の悪化を低減することに役立つものであり、さらには、省エネにつながることに関するものである。

【考案の概要】

【考案が解決しようとする課題】

【０００２】

カーテンやブラインドや簾等を用いて直射日光の室内への照射を遮り、室内への温度環境の悪化を防止している。しかし、それだけでは遮きれない放射熱や輻射熱が室内への温度環境を悪化させ、エアコン等の電力に負荷をかけている。

【０００３】

また、外気による熱気や冷気の影響が室内への寒暖に影響し、温度環境を悪化させ、室内の冷房や暖房のための手段を取らざるを得ないような状況になっている。

【課題を解決するための手段】

【０００４】

本考案は、雨戸やガラス戸や障子戸等の居住側の空きスペースを有効活用して、該雨戸や該ガラス戸や該障子戸等の枠に囲まれた凹み面に断熱体をはめ込むことにより、室内の温度環境の悪化を低減させることを特徴とする遮蔽形体。

【考案の効果】

【０００５】

断熱体が有する熱気や冷気を遮蔽する効果を利用することにより、室内への温度環境の悪化を低減させることに役立つ。

【０００６】

また朝夕の日差しの移動や外気温の変化に応じて、該雨戸や該ガラス戸や該障子戸

の開け閉めが自由にでき、室内の温度環境の調節が簡便にできる。

【図面の簡単な説明】

【0007】

【図1】雨戸に断熱体をはめ込んだ実施例の正面図である。

【図2】ガラス戸に断熱体をはめ込んだ実施例の正面図である。

【図3】障子戸に断熱体をはめ込んだ実施例の正面図である。

【符号の説明】

【0008】

1　断熱体

2　雨戸ロック部の断熱体の切り欠き部分

3　ガラス

4　断熱体支持具

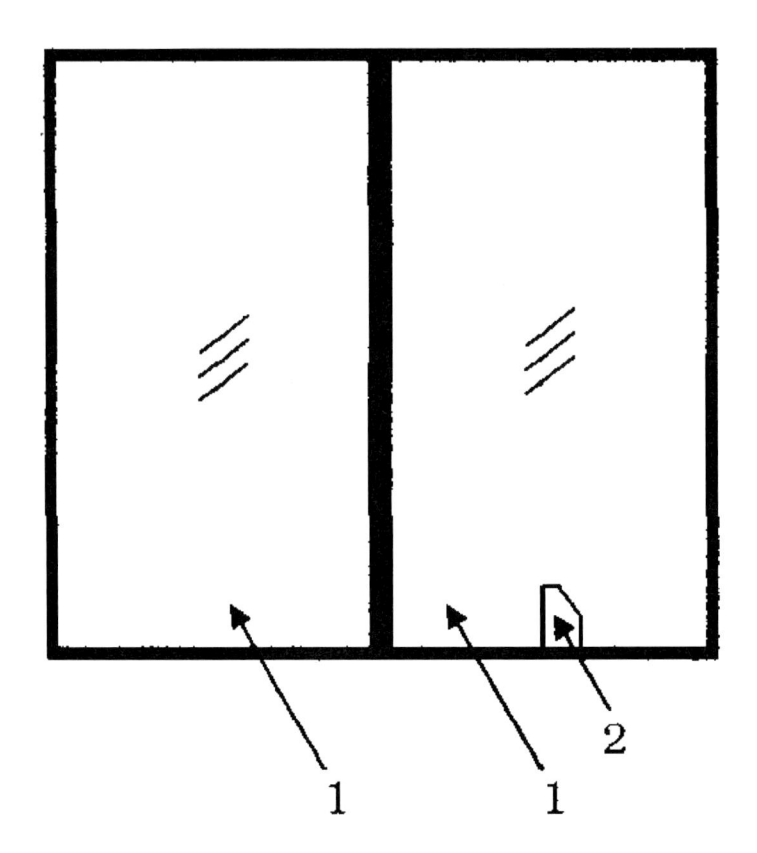

【図1】

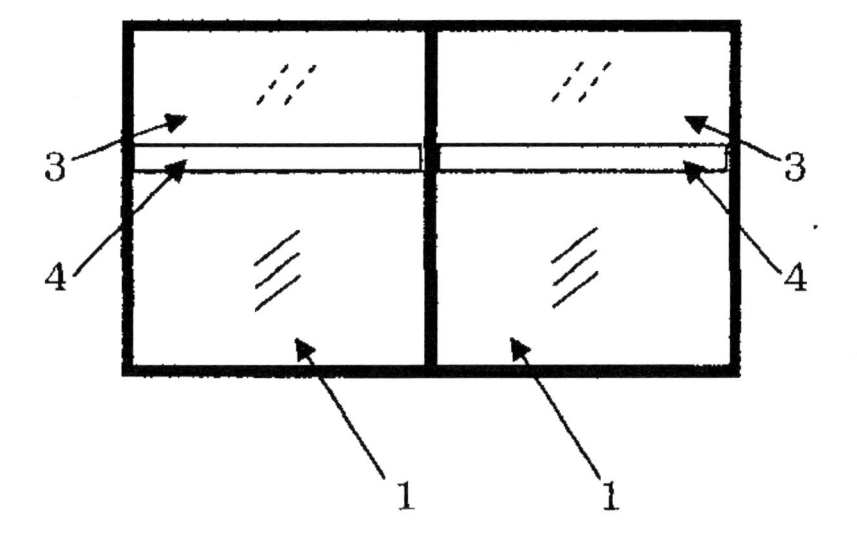

【図2】

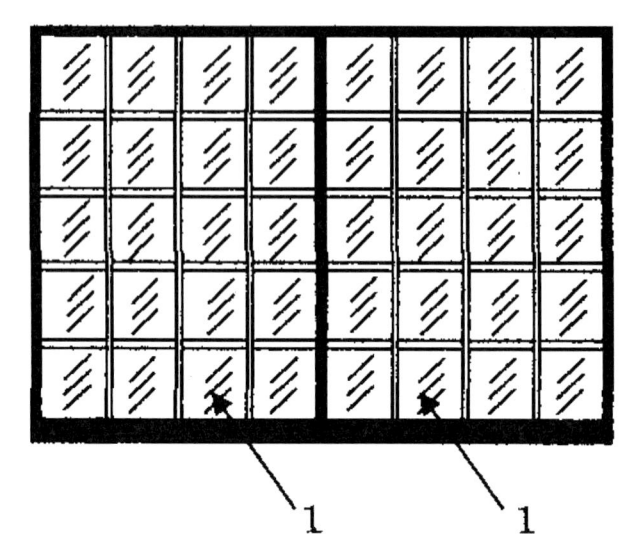

【図3】

1
1

5、Patent journal English

DETAILED DESCRIPTION

[Detailed explanation of the device]

[Application of the Invention]

[0001]

This design is utility preventing a shade, heat, cold, etc. and reducing aggravation of indoor temperature environment.

It is related with leading to energy saving.

[The outline of a device]

[Problem(s) to be Solved by the Device]

[0002]

The exposure to the interior of a room of direct sunlight was interrupted using a curtain, a blind, **, etc., and aggravation of the temperature environment to the interior of a room is prevented. However, only by it, the radiant heat and the radiant heat which are not in ****** worsened the temperature environment to the interior of a room, and have applied load to electric power, such as an air-conditioner.

[0003]

The influence of the heat by the open air or cold influences the temperature to the interior of a room, and worsens temperature environment, and it has become a situation where the means for indoor air conditioning or heating must be taken.

[Means for solving problem]

[0004]

A shielding form, wherein this design reduces aggravation of indoor temperature environment by using effectively the free space by the side of habitation of a sliding shutter, a glass door, a sash door, etc., and inserting a heat-insulating element in the dent surface surrounded by frames, such as this sliding shutter, this glass door, and this sash door.

[Effect of the Device]

[0005]

By using the effect which shields the heat which a heat-insulating element has, and cold, it is useful to reduce aggravation of the temperature environment to the interior of a room.

[0006]

According to movement of the sunlight of every morning and evening, or change of outside air temperature, opening and closing of this sliding shutter, this glass door, and this sash door can be performed freely, and regulation of indoor temperature environment can be performed simple.

[Brief Description of the Drawings]

[0007]

[Drawing 1]It is a front view of the working example which inserted the heat-insulating element in the sliding shutter.

[Drawing 2]It is a front view of the working example which inserted the heat-insulating element in the glass door.

[Drawing 3]It is a front view of the working example which inserted the heat-insulating element in the sash door.

[Explanations of letters or numerals]

[0008]

1 Heat-insulating element

2 The notching portion of the heat-insulating element of a sliding shutter lock part

3 Glass

4 Heat-insulating element support

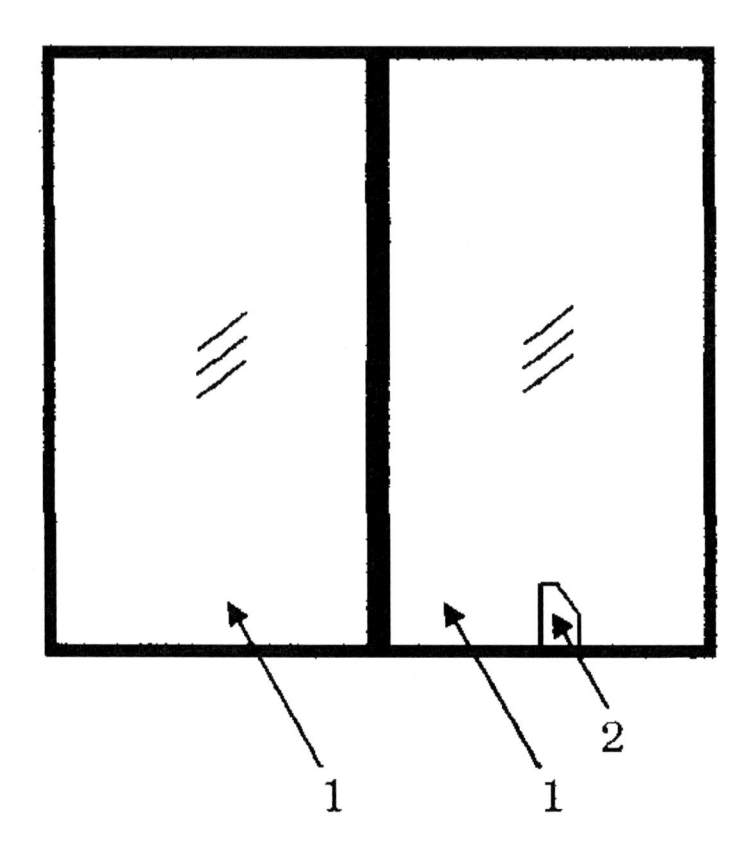

[Drawing 1]

1 1 2

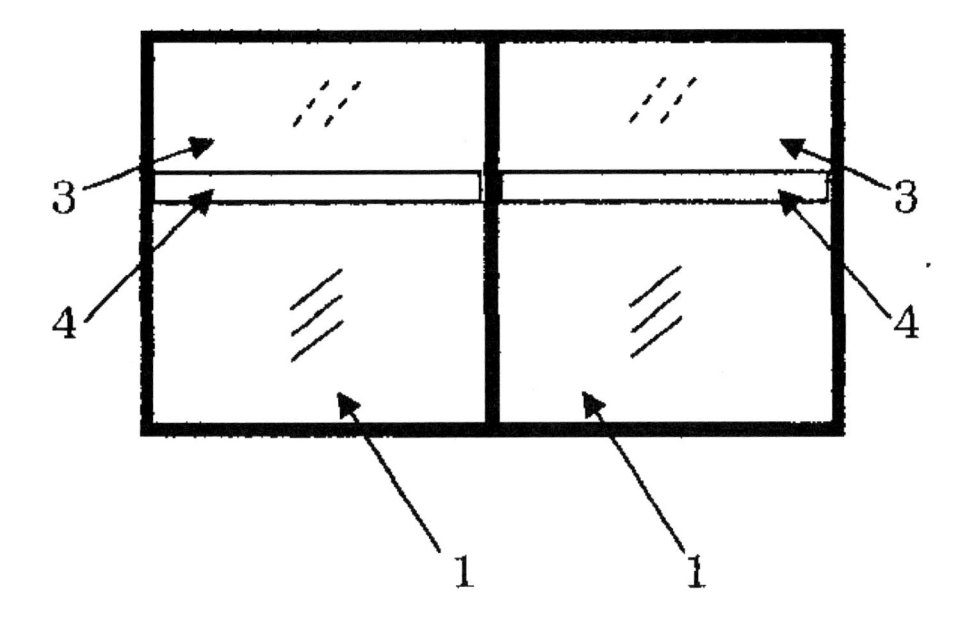

[Drawing 2]

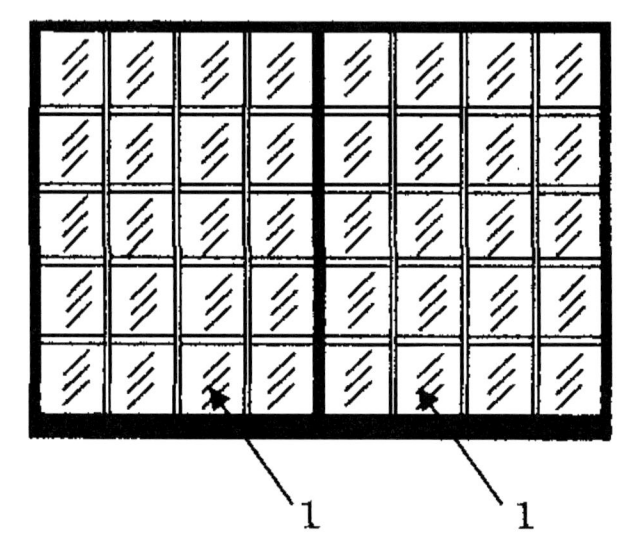

[Drawing 3]

嵌め込み式遮蔽形体の用途解説

定価（本体 1,500 円＋税）

―――――――――――――――――――――――――――――――

２０１４年（平成２６年）７月１０日発行

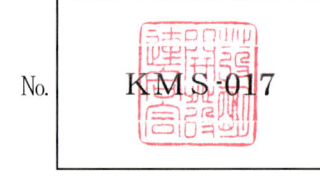

No. KMS-017

発行所　IDF（INVENTION DEVLOPMENT FEDERATION）
　　　　発明開発連合会®
メール 03-3498@idf-0751.com　www.idf-0751.com
電話 03-3498-0751㈹
150-8691 渋谷郵便局私書箱第２５８号
発行人　ましば寿一
著作権企画　IDF 発明開発(連)
Printed in Japan
著者　小松省司 ©
　　　　（コマツショウジ）

―――――――――――――――――――――――――――――――

本書の一部または全部を無断で複写、複製、転載、データーファイル化することを禁じています。

It forbids a copy, a duplicate, reproduction, and forming a data file for some or all of this book without notice.